GOING PLACES

CHILDREN LIVING WITH CEREBRAL PALSY

DON'T
TURN
AWAY

For a free color catalog describing Gareth Stevens' list of high-quality children's books, call 1-800-341-3569 (USA) or 1-800-461-9120 (Canada).

Don't Turn Away
Going Places: Children Living with Cerebral Palsy
Finding a Common Language: Children Living with Deafness
One Day at a Time: Children Living with Leukemia
Seeing in Special Ways: Children Living with Blindness
We Laugh, We Love, We Cry: Children Living with Mental Retardation
On Our Own Terms: Children Living with Physical Disabilities

The editors gratefully thank Joyce Altman, executive director, and Tom Hlavacek, program director, of United Cerebral Palsy of Southeastern Wisconsin, Inc., for their enthusiastic encouragement and technical assistance.

Library of Congress Cataloging-in-Publication Data

Bergman, Thomas, 1947-
    [Kul på hjul med Mathias. English]
    Going places : children living with cerebral palsy / Thomas Bergman. — 1st North American ed.
        p.   cm. — (Don't turn away)
    Translation of: Kul på hjul med Mathias
    Includes bibliographical references and index.
    ISBN 0-8368-0199-7
    1. Cerebral palsy—Juvenile literature. 2. Cerebral palsied children—Juvenile literature. I. Title.
II. Series: Bergman, Thomas, 1947- Don't turn away.
RJ496.C4B4513   1991
362.1'9892836—dc20

90-48266

D O N 'T

T U R N

A W A Y

North American edition first published in 1991 by

Gareth Stevens Children's Books
1555 North RiverCenter Drive, Suite 201
Milwaukee, Wisconsin 53212, USA

First published in Sweden in 1990 by Rabén and Sjögren under the title *Kul på hjul med Mathias.*

Project editor: Carolyn Kott Washburne
Series designer: Kate Kriege
Layout designer: Kristi Ludwig

Printed in the United States of America

2 3 4 5 6 7 8 9 97 96 95 94 93

GOING PLACES

CHILDREN LIVING WITH CEREBRAL PALSY

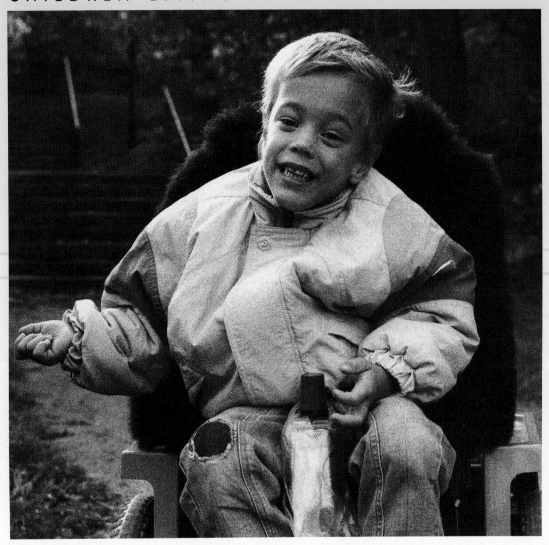

Thomas Bergman

Gareth Stevens Children's Books
MILWAUKEE

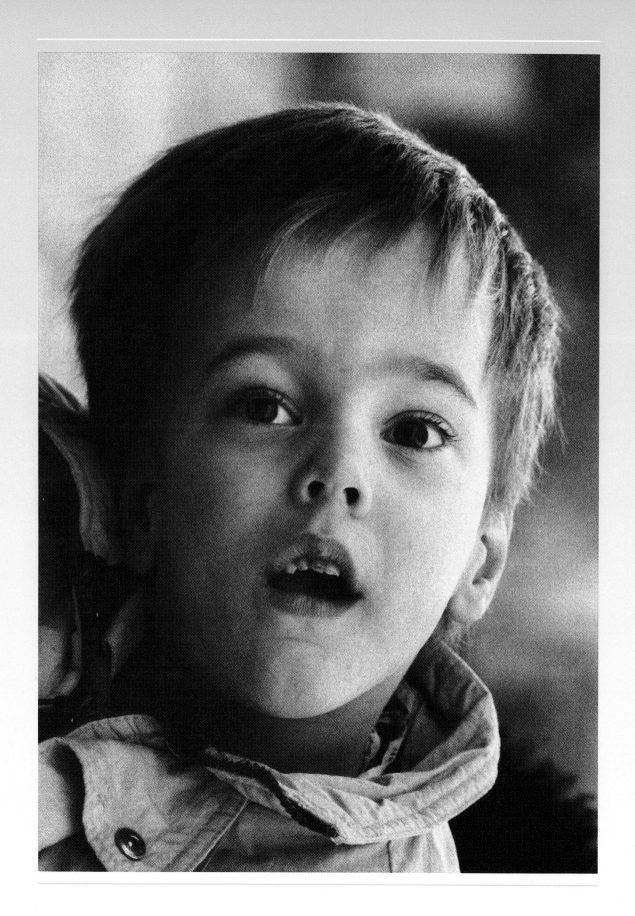

In Going Places *you will meet Mathias, a courageous boy with many interests and activities. Mathias calls upon his courage every day to do what other children can do with much less effort. Mathias has cerebral palsy, a condition that makes it hard for him to learn how to use his muscles.*

The unforgettable photographs in this book were taken by Thomas Bergman, an internationally known photographer. He also wrote the text, and his words reveal his sensitivity and compassion for children who have physical disabilities.

As you share Mathias' life in the pages of this book, you will find that he has qualities that are similar to and different from those of other children. Thomas' photographs and text dramatize the strength and determination that so many children have. Let Mathias show you that a disability can bring opportunities to share the hopes and disappointments, the struggles and dreams of all of us.

Gareth Stevens
Gareth Stevens
PUBLISHER

In this book we get to know Mathias, a charming six-year-old boy who has had cerebral palsy from birth. As a result of this early injury to the brain, he has a serious physical disability and must use a wheelchair. Furthermore, he is almost totally deaf. Mathias needs a lot of practice to learn things that children without disabilities learn easily. For example, it took him five years to be able to crawl.

I followed Mathias for six months. We were constantly on the go, spending time at his home, at school, and at his physical therapist's. At preschool, I saw him playing and learning sign language with other children who are deaf and hearing-impaired.

I hope my words and photographs will show what an exciting and interesting life Mathias lives and how his progress pleases him and his family. Like most people with cerebral palsy, Mathias is capable of accomplishing a great deal. With the education and adaptive equipment available today, his future looks bright indeed.

Thomas Bergman
Thomas Bergman

MATHIAS

This is Mathias sitting in his electric wheelchair. He is six years old. The others in his family are his mother, his father, and his younger sister Emma. They all talk with each other using sign language. The family's cat is named Smulan.

Mathias was born three months too early. He weighed less than three pounds. During those first weeks, he was so seriously ill that he could not breathe or eat by himself. He lived in an incubator, where he was cared for. He was bathed in a small bowl.

After eight months, Mathias still could not lift his head or sit or crawl. The doctors diagnosed him as having cerebral palsy.

"When Mathias was two years old, we were told that, besides having cerebral palsy, he was almost totally deaf," says Mathias' mother. "At first we despaired. But Mathias himself was so happy, and he had such a strong will. That made everything so much easier for us."

Mathias lives with his family in a four-room apartment. He has a room of his own, where he keeps his toys and other personal treasures. He also has a typing telephone. This is like a typewriter, with the words coming out on a screen. Every time the telephone rings, lights twinkle all over the apartment. Mathias' mother holds him on her lap so he can get close enough to reach the keys.

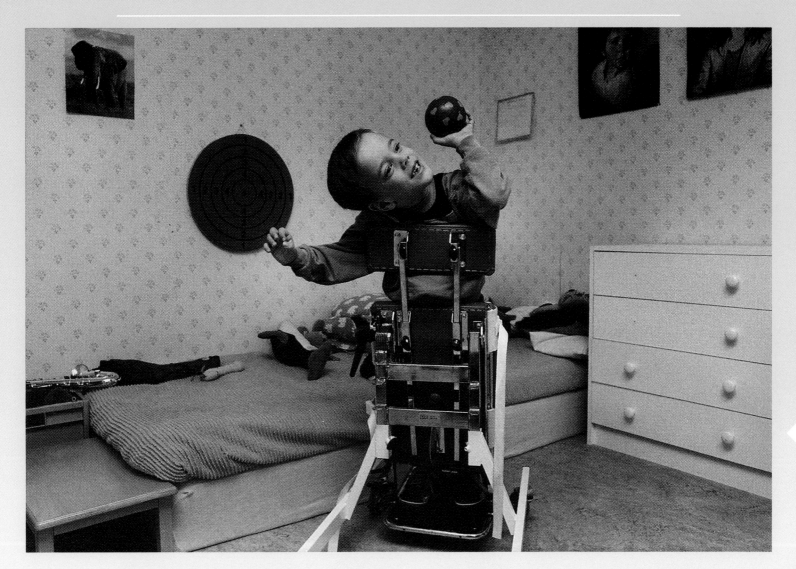

Every day, Mathias practices standing up. He supports himself with a standing frame and tries to hold his head straight all by himself. Since he enjoys himself, this is not hard practice. He throws the ball to his mother, but he is not so good at catching it yet.

Mathias did not learn to crawl until he was five years old. He must struggle for everything new that he learns.

When Mathias crawls toward the record player, his mother knows he wants
her to play a record with rock music. It should have a lot of bass sound
because that's what he likes. Mathias claims that he hears the music, but he
is really feeling the vibrations from the loudspeakers. He pretends to play
the guitar, using a tennis racket.

Emma comes in carrying the cat. The cat thinks Mathias is playing too loud
and disappears into the bedroom and under the bed.

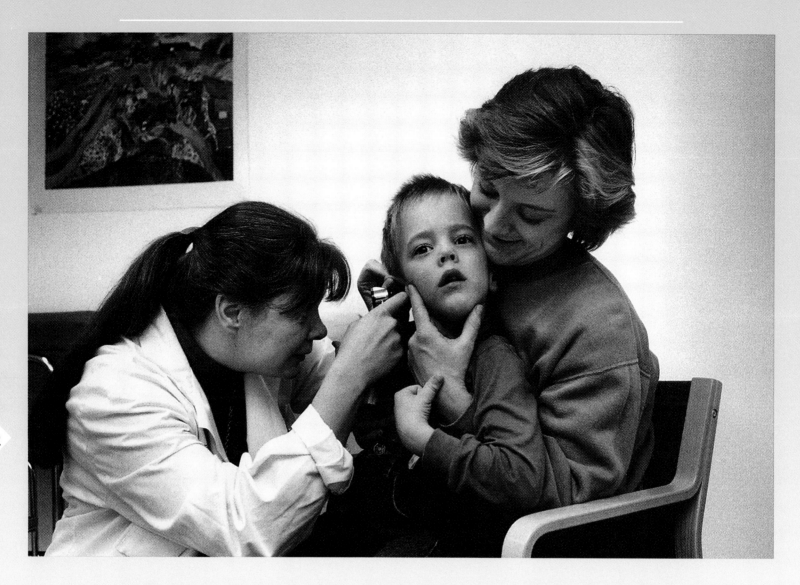

Now and then Mathias has to go to the doctor. His mother goes with him. His doctor is named Mia, and they have known each other for several years. Mia sees to it that Mathias gets all the extra help he needs.

Today Mia examines Mathias' ears because they hurt. Then he wants to look in Mia's ears. Mathias has a hearing aid to help him hear deep bass tones. But usually the hearing aid makes everything too noisy, and he does not want to wear it.

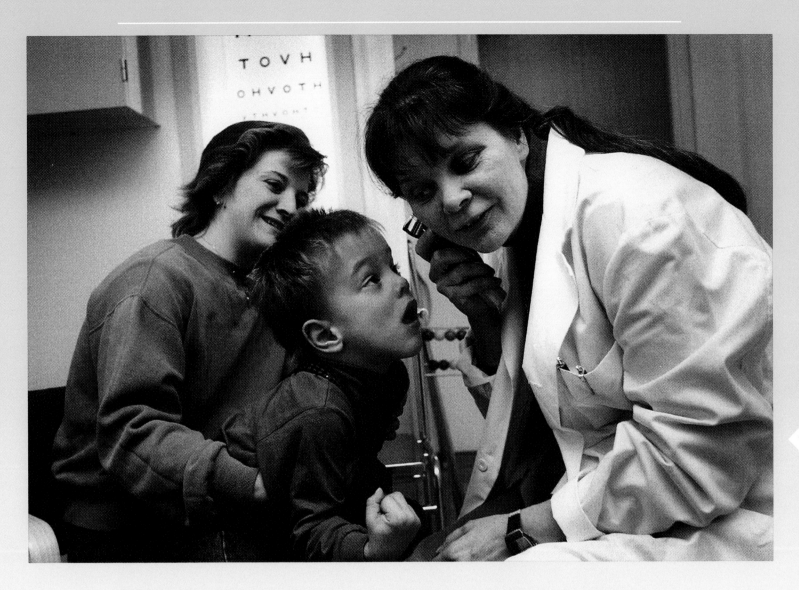

Mia also examines his reflexes and checks how he moves. She hopes Mathias will learn to stand up and walk, supported by braces and a roller he can push in front of him. His right arm is often bent upward. He also finds it difficult to keep his head straight. At the physical therapist's, he must practice keeping his balance and unbending his arm.

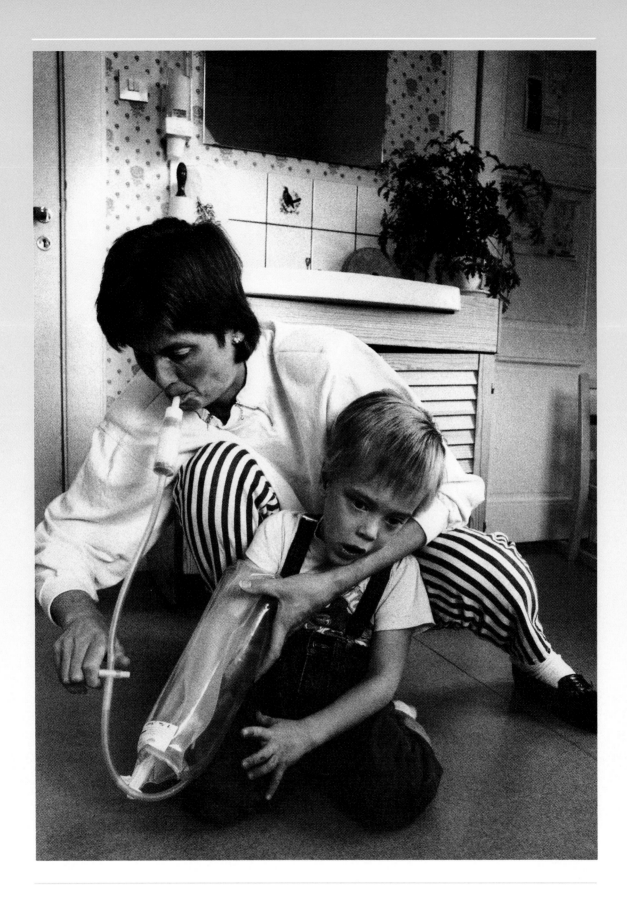

Mathias' physical therapist is Eva. She is training Mathias to improve his
balance and his control over his body. She puts an inflated plastic bag on
his arm. This helps him straighten his arm, even if it is only for a short
while. Then, supported by a rounded cushion, he tries to find a good
sitting position. He is supposed to lean back and then try to sit up again.

Mathias finds it hard to control his arms and legs by himself. Sometimes
when he crawls, he falls down and hits his chin on the floor.

Mathias also works with Barbara, his speech therapist. She is helping him develop better language skills. He can only say "Mom" and "Dad" and a few other words. He can understand people when they sign to him, but it is difficult for him to sign because he can only use one of his hands.

Mathias is doing a jigsaw puzzle where the different pieces have handles, and he does it quickly.

Barbara takes out a toy chair and a teddy bear. She signs to Mathias to put the bear under the chair, and he does that. She also shows him different pictures, and now she holds up a picture of a tiger. Barbara wants Mathias to sign what the picture shows.

Even if Mathias has seen a tiger before in a picture or at the zoo, he finds it hard to explain what kind of animal it is, or if it is wild or tame. He must look at the picture often and have it explained more than once.

For half an hour each week, Mathias practices on a computer. He has done this for several months now and likes it very much. His teacher is Gunnar, who has worked for many years with children who have disabilities.

Gunnar says, "Asking is the way a child gets to know the world. Children who cannot speak cannot ask. Sign language is very useful, but not everyone has the opportunity to learn it."

Gunnar also says that Mathias needs computer training. He knows the whole alphabet, and, with assistance, he can already write entire sentences. He usually manages to write nine or ten sentences each time. Gunnar wishes that they could have more time together to practice on the computer because there is so much Mathias needs to learn. When he starts school, the computer will help him with both writing and counting.

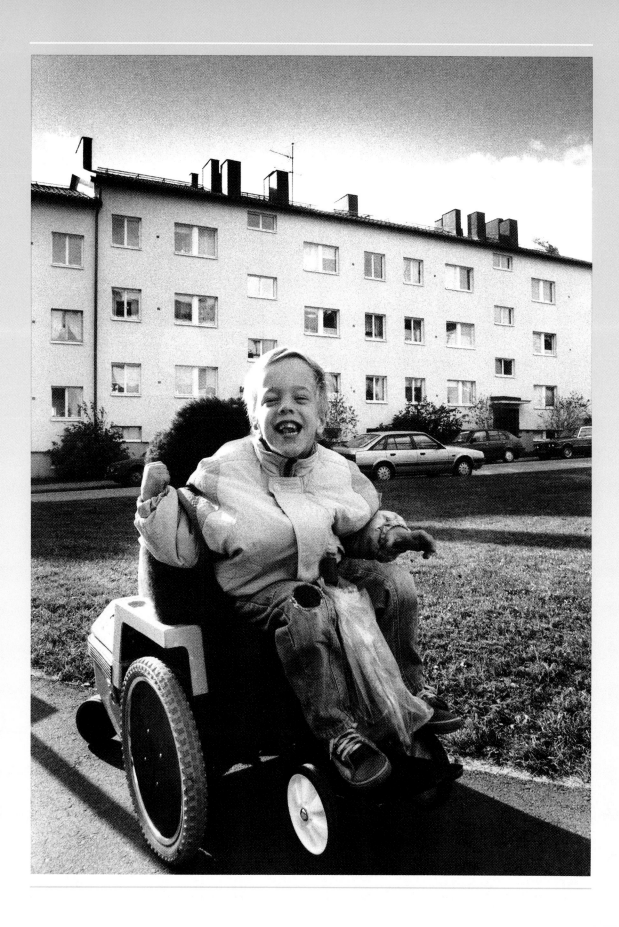

Mathias' mother says his life changed completely when he got his electric wheelchair. It was built especially for him, and he can drive it while both sitting and standing. With a single lever, Mathias can steer it forward or backward and turn in any direction. The wheelchair is like his legs — it means freedom. Now he can get where he wants all by himself.

"Before, we used to drive Mathias around, but now he fools us and just takes off," his mother says. "When we run after him, he turns around. His eyes are sparkling, and he is laughing at us."

Emma and Mathias often play together. Emma has learned some sign language, so she and Mathias can understand each other.

Their mother is in the kitchen preparing dough because the children want to make cinnamon buns. They both knead the dough. Mathias wants to make big buns with lots of cinnamon in them. It turns out there are not as many buns as they expected because Emma and Mathias like to taste the dough. Mathias prefers to use his left arm when he rolls out the dough. It is quicker that way. But he needs to use his right arm to help make the rest of his body steadier.

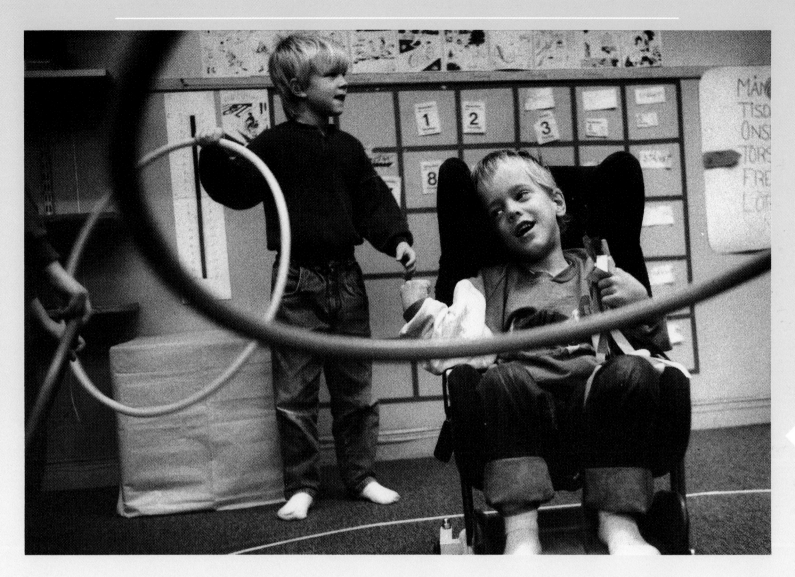

Four days a week, Mathias goes to his preschool. He is the only child there who has cerebral palsy. Some of the children there are deaf or have hearing impairments. They talk to each other using sign language. There are also children without disabilities at the preschool.

Today the parents are coming to watch the children and teacher play circus. Mathias is supposed to be a horse. Others are lions or acrobats. One girl is a clown. The children enjoy themselves very much, and the parents are very proud of them. After the performance, coffee, lemonade, and ice-cream cake are served.

Once a week, Mathias goes to a different school. There, he and other children practice moving around in their wheelchairs. Mathias and two other children have electric wheelchairs. When they first arrive, all of the children get together in a ring for physical exercises.

Mathias practices driving between cone-shaped markers. Like a slalom skier, he moves forward, turns, and then moves back, weaving in and out between the markers. Mathias loves this challenge and wants to do even harder exercises. These activities will prepare the children for getting around in different places.

Mathias and the other children who have difficulty moving their arms are playing with a balloon. Mathias hits the balloon to Emily, who hits it to Christopher. Children on wheels have fun, and Mathias' friends at the preschool who are not disabled are a little jealous of him. Sometimes Mathias lets them go for a ride with him.

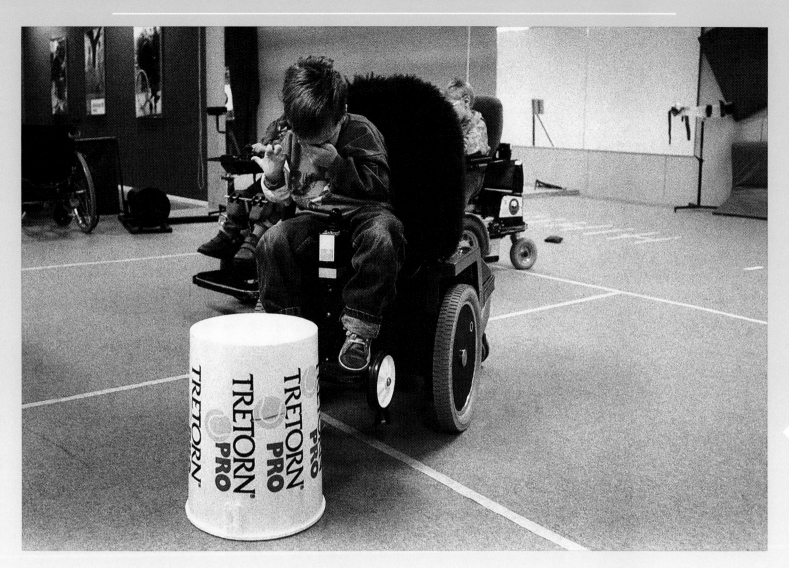

Children using wheelchairs, whether electric or regular, are able to play most of the same games as everyone else. Today they want to play hide-and-seek. Mathias sits, counting, while the others try to hide.

Mathias is busy every day of the week. On Fridays he goes to horseback-riding school with his mother and Mio, who sometimes helps him. Today at the school, there are five other children who have disabilities, too. The horse Mathias will ride is almost all black. Mio helps Mathias saddle it.

The children mount with help from the grown-ups working in the stable. Mathias can sit by himself, but he feels safer when his mother gently holds his leg. He gets steadier and more upright as he rides.

The children also get a little physical training on horseback. One exercise is trying to reach the horse's ears. The children usually ride for an hour, but Mathias' bottom is hurting, so he wants to stop earlier. He usually brings an apple for the horse because he knows that the horse likes apples.

Mathias has been asking all morning about going ice-skating, so his mother
takes him to a nearby ice rink. He has gone skating before, with his mother
and father holding him on each side. Now he has brought his walker.
Because it is on wheels, he does not need any help. He skates by himself
by pushing with his skates and then gliding forward with the walker.

The ice is somewhat bumpy, but Mathias enjoys himself anyway. He skates quite well and is proud that he hardly ever falls down. After a while, his skates start pinching. Then Mathias thinks he has had enough this time and asks to go home.

On most Sundays, several children with disabilities gather at a swimming pool, together with their parents, brothers, and sisters. "Getting together with others who are in the same situation means so much to us," says Mathias' father.

Mathias becomes very lively in the pool. He feels he can move better in the water. Everyone is in the pool with the children, who are learning to relax and get used to the water. Ake, the teacher, sings, and everyone moves around in a circle, holding hands. They play and have a good time.

The children learn to float, dip their heads, and blow bubbles in the water. Mathias blows on a Ping-Pong ball and watches it move. It is good practice for him to hold up his head and use his arms and legs. These exercises teach him to feel confident being in the water by himself. Later on, he will learn to swim alone.

A game called "The Bear Is Sleeping" usually ends the swimming lessons. Today, Emma is the bear sleeping in her grandmother's arms.

After swimming, their father asks Mathias and Emma if they want to go to the city by subway to have a hamburger. Mathias signs with all his body that he would like to very much. Going by subway is great, he thinks. Most of all, he loves to go into the subway tunnel. He laughs and signs that he wants to go far under the earth.

At the restaurant, Mathias first wants to go around and watch the other children eating. Then he orders two hamburgers with ketchup and french fries. When his mother, father, and Emma have all ordered, Mathias pays the bill by himself with his father's money. Mathias quickly eats both his hamburgers, but Emma only eats half of hers. The lemonade is taking up too much room in her stomach. After the meal, they take the subway back home. Both children are very tired.

Soon Mathias will enter school. Because he has both a physical disability and a hearing impairment, it is hard to know which school will be best for him. He would like to join his friends from the preschool entering the school for children who are deaf. But Mathias needs to improve his sign language before he can go there.

Mathias needs a school where the grown-ups will work to help him make the most of his talents and develop his potential. Mathias also needs to get a computer of his own to practice on and play with. Mathias' father works with computers, too. He hopes that someday the two of them will be able to solve problems together.

Mathias is very proud of all the new things he has learned. "We have learned a lot, too," his father says. "We are very grateful for that. And we are very proud of Mathias."

41

QUESTIONS FROM CHILDREN ABOUT CEREBRAL PALSY

Getting the answers to questions is one way of gaining more understanding about people with cerebral palsy. Here are some of the most frequent questions that children ask.

What is cerebral palsy?
Cerebral palsy is a condition caused by damage to the brain. "Cerebral" refers to the brain, and "palsy" means a disorder of movement or posture. The condition usually occurs before, during, or just after birth and is among the most common birth disabilities.

How do doctors know whether a child has cerebral palsy?
The symptoms of cerebral palsy vary widely, depending on the severity and location of the brain damage. Some children with cerebral palsy may show no obvious signs for a long time. Others may have serious symptoms from birth.

What are the symptoms?
The physical symptoms that a baby may have are difficulty in sucking, poor muscle control, and poor coordination, such as having trouble picking up and holding a toy. The physical symptoms can also include muscle spasms and seizures or problems with seeing and hearing. The behavioral symptoms are unusual tenseness, inability to concentrate, and emotional problems.

Are people who have cerebral palsy mentally retarded?
Having cerebral palsy does not mean being mentally retarded. Cerebral palsy has to do mainly with difficulties in controlling muscles. Mental retardation is a different condition. A very small number of people with cerebral palsy may also have some mental retardation, but the two conditions are not related.

What are the causes of cerebral palsy?
There are many causes. The brain can be damaged before birth if the mother uses drugs or alcohol, or has certain diseases, for example, German measles. Brain damage can also result if the unborn baby does not get enough oxygen, or if the baby is born prematurely.

Another cause can be when the Rh factors in the blood of both mother and child are incompatible, or in conflict. This happens when the mother has Rh negative blood and the baby she is carrying has Rh positive blood. The mother's blood develops antibodies that can attack the baby's red blood cells. The breakdown products of these damaged red blood cells can injure the baby's brain. The mother's doctor can help prevent this from happening, but this condition must be detected ahead of time. Usually the first baby is not harmed by the mother's antibodies. About 15 percent of the population has blood that is Rh negative.

Cerebral palsy can also result if the brain is damaged early in life due to accidental injury, an illness such as meningitis, lead poisoning, or repeated shaking or beating of the child.

Can I catch cerebral palsy?
No. It is not a disease, and you can't catch or inherit it. Also, it is not progressive, meaning that the condition does not get worse. On the other hand, cerebral palsy cannot be cured, although therapy and sometimes surgery can help.

If cerebral palsy can't be cured, why treat it?
"Management" is a better word than "treatment." Management consists of helping the child reach his or her maximum potential for growth and development. Therapy should be started early to help the child live as fully as possible in our society.

Medication can help control seizures or muscle spasms. Surgery may correct difficulties in seeing, hearing, and walking. Occupational therapy helps with coordination and learning daily routines such as eating and writing. Physical therapy helps a child get stronger and use adaptive equipment such as braces, walkers, page turners, specially equipped cars, and motorized wheelchairs. Counseling can be useful for both the child and the family to help with the emotional, social, and practical problems of having a disability.

How many people have cerebral palsy?
Experts estimate that between 500,000 and 700,000 children and adults in the United States have one or more of the symptoms of cerebral palsy.

Can cerebral palsy be prevented?
Yes. Expectant mothers can take good care of themselves before and during pregnancy. This means developing habits of good nutrition and exercise before pregnancy and getting regular checkups during pregnancy. One of those checkups should include a test for the Rh factor.

If Rh incompatibility exists and if this is the mother's first baby, the doctor can give the mother medication to keep her blood from forming harmful antibodies against her baby's blood. If the mother's blood already has formed antibodies because she has had another baby before this one, the doctor can plan an exchange transfusion as soon as the new baby is born.

During the exchange transfusion, the baby's blood, containing the mother's harmful antibodies, is taken out at the same time that donated blood is put in. The blood that the baby's body continues to make after this will not have any of the mother's harmful antibodies in it.

After birth, every baby should have regular check-ups, eat healthy foods, and get immunized against childhood diseases. The family can also take safety precautions and avoid accidents.

What programs help people with cerebral palsy?
The largest organization is United Cerebral Palsy, a nationwide network of about 190 state and local agencies. United Cerebral Palsy provides services to people with cerebral palsy, conducts programs to educate the public, and sponsors research. It was founded in 1948, and many of its founders were parents of children with cerebral palsy.

How can research help?
Scientists, doctors, and therapists continue to make impressive strides through research. Important advances have been made in

- **prevention**, such as immunizations against viruses and improvements in health care for both mothers and children;

- **detection**, such as early identification of babies with brain damage and better techniques for testing the learning potential of children with cerebral palsy;

- **treatment**, such as drug research to find effective, safe medicines to relieve the symptoms of cerebral palsy, research into ways of regenerating the central nervous system, and improved mechanical aids; and

- **services**, such as improved education and job training programs, as well as better foster care and day care centers.

We can all help by accepting people with cerebral palsy in our schools, our neighborhoods, and our work places, just as we accept people without cerebral palsy.

Are there any words I shouldn't use when talking about people with cerebral palsy?
Yes. There are words people use without thinking that offend persons with cerebral palsy and their families and friends. Careless words hurt because they are negative, or just plain wrong.

The word "afflicted," for example, is very negative. It is much better to say "a person who has cerebral palsy" or "someone with cerebral palsy." Avoid saying "crippled." This word carries a mental picture of a limited existence. But people with cerebral palsy are leading busy lives that are filled with many interests and activities.

The phrase "suffers from" doesn't apply if the person is independent and copes with life as well as most of us, so this phrase is wrong. And the word "victim" is not correct when used for people who have cerebral palsy. "Victim" refers to people injured or killed in some accident or circumstance, like a car crash or a burning house.

Never use the word "spastic" when referring to people with cerebral palsy. Muscles may be spastic, but people never are.

What will children with cerebral palsy do when they grow up? Where will they live?
People with cerebral palsy want the same things as everyone else when they grow up. Many will work in regular jobs in the community. There are many doctors, lawyers, accountants, actors, and engineers who have cerebral palsy. Some people will need extra training and support to be productive workers. Sheltered workshops are places where some people with more severe cerebral palsy can get the extra training they need.

Many adults with cerebral palsy are married and have families of their own. Most young adults with cerebral palsy want to move out on their own and can live in apartments or houses. Some people will continue to live at home with their parents or might live in an institution, such as a nursing home.

Remember, people with cerebral palsy have the same goals as people everywhere. They want to get the most from life, and they want to achieve independence and a sense of personal worth. They want to make friends, get a good education, and have fun. And they want a chance for satisfying employment and to be productive, contributing citizens, just like everyone else.

THINGS TO DO AND THINK ABOUT

These projects will help you understand more about living with cerebral palsy.

1. Learn more about disabilities. Invite members of organizations for people with disabilities to speak at your school, church, or synagogue. Send for written information. Volunteer with an organization that helps people who have disabilities.

2. Understand your own attitudes about disabilities by asking yourself these questions: Do you know anyone who has a disability? What is your first memory of that person? Do you remember what you thought and felt about that person? Was the person treated any differently from others? By whom? How do you think it would feel if you were different?

3. Be sensitive and aware when you are around someone who uses a wheelchair. Here are some guidelines: The person in a wheelchair is in the best position to know what activities to participate in, so trust that person's judgment. Do not hold onto the wheelchair — it is part of the person's body space. Offer assistance if you wish, but do not insist. Talk directly to the person, not to a third party. He or she is not helpless or unable to communicate with you. If your conversation goes for more than a few minutes, think about sitting down in order to share eye level. A seated person finds it uncomfortable to look straight up for a long period. If you are curious, go ahead and ask appropriate questions, but don't pry. Use good judgment. Many people will welcome your interest and will want to answer questions to dispel myths about their disability.

4. Look around your school or neighborhood for people with disabilities at work. How many are there? What do they do? Ask one or two of them if they are willing to be interviewed by you. Here are some questions you might ask: How did you decide to do this type of job? How were you trained for it?

What do you like best about your job? Least? How do you get back and forth to work? Is there any special equipment you need to do your job? What are your goals? Write up your interview in a report or letter to a friend.

5. Analyze how accessible your school is for someone who uses a wheelchair or walker. Make a list of the possible barriers. These could be stairs, narrow aisles between the desks, narrow doorways, and high drinking fountains, pencil sharpeners, and bookshelves. Make a report on the barriers you find, and list your suggestions for eliminating them. Present your report to the principal.

6. Arrange to tour a new building that is barrier-free. Ask about and write down all the ways the building has been made accessible to someone who uses a wheelchair. Some of these ways are parking spaces reserved for people with disabilities, ramps to the main entrance, doorknobs three feet (91.4 cm) from the ground, handrails in the hallways, doorways to bathrooms at least 33 inches (84 cm) wide, and low sinks and telephones. What are some of the things that people who use wheelchairs or walkers could do more easily in that building than in buildings that have barriers? What ideas do you have about how older buildings could be changed?

7. More than anything else, look for what you have in common with people who have disabilities, not how you are different.

45

WHERE TO WRITE FOR FURTHER INFORMATION

The people at these organizations will send you free information about living with cerebral palsy and other physical disabilities if you write to them. Some of the organizations have state and local offices as well as the national ones listed here. If they're listed in your phone book, you can give them a call. Some of them offer programs just for children and will send someone to talk to your class or group. Whether writing or calling, give them your reason for wanting the information so they can send you material that suits your purpose.

Canadian Association for Community Living
Kinsmen Building, York University
4700 Keele Street
Downsview, Ontario M3J 1P3

Canadian Cerebral Palsy Association
880 Wellington Street, Suite 612
Ottawa, Ontario K1R 6K7

Center for Independent Living
2539 Telegraph Avenue
Berkeley, CA 94704

March of Dimes Birth Defects Foundation
1275 Mamaroneck Avenue
White Plains, NY 10605

National Easter Seal Society
70 East Lake Street
Chicago, IL 60601

National Wheelchair Athletic Association
3595 East Fountain Boulevard, Suite L-10
Colorado Springs, CO   80910

TASH: The Association for Persons with
    Severe Handicaps
7010 Roosevelt Way NE
Seattle, WA 98115

United Cerebral Palsy Associations, Inc.
7 Penn Plaza, Suite 804
New York, NY 10001
1-800-USA-lUCP (1-800-872-1827)

MORE BOOKS ABOUT CHILDREN AND PHYSICAL DISABILITIES

The children in the books listed below have physical disabilities. You may be surprised at how much their dreams and feelings are like yours.

About Handicaps. Stein (Walker)
Computers for the Disabled. Cattoche (Franklin Watts)
The Discovery Book: A Helpful Guide for the World Written by Children with Disabilities. Chaney and Fisher (United Cerebral Palsy Association of the North Bay)
Don't Feel Sorry for Paul. Wolf (Harper & Row Jr. Bks.)
Finding a Common Language: Children Living with Deafness. Bergman (Gareth Stevens)
Karen. Killilea (Dell)
Margaret Moves. Rabe (Dutton)

On Our Own Terms: Children Living with Physical Disabilities. Bergman (Gareth Stevens)
Please Don't Tease Me. Madsen (Judson)
A Show of Hands: Say It in Sign Language. Sullivan (Harper & Row Junior Books)
Ted Kennedy Jr.: He Faced His Challenge. Martin (Rourke)
The Value of Facing a Challenge: The Story of Terry Fox. Johnson (Oak Tree)
What Is the Sign for Friend? Greenberg (Franklin Watts)

GLOSSARY OF WORDS ABOUT CEREBRAL PALSY

The terms listed below will help you learn more about physical disabilities, their effects on the body, and their treatment.

acquired disability: a condition that results from an injury or illness, rather than a condition that occurred before birth.

adaptive equipment: equipment that helps someone with a disability function fully in daily life; this equipment includes braces, walkers, page turners, specially equipped cars, motorized wheelchairs, and computers.

atrophy: to weaken or to waste away to the point of uselessness. This can happen to muscles if they are not used, for example, after an injury.

brain damage: a defect of the brain that prevents a person from doing certain things, like moving, thinking, seeing, or hearing.

congenital disability: a condition a person has from birth that limits the ability to do something.

developmental disability: a kind of disability that limits how much a person will learn and how fast he or she will develop.

early intervention: the practice of educating children from the time somebody notices their disability, right after birth if possible. The idea behind this practice is that valuable learning time is lost if therapies and programs for learning are delayed until the time when a child would normally start school. Children who receive early intervention start school with more of the skills of other children their age.

impairment: loss of strength, feeling, or the ability to move.

integration: *see* **mainstreaming**.

mainstreaming: teaching children with disabilities and children without them together. Mainstreaming is sometimes called school integration. It replaced the older system that put children with disabilities in classes and schools by themselves. All children today can learn more about themselves and others by sharing the same classroom.

multiple disabilities: more than one disability in a person. Mathias, for example, has both cerebral palsy and a hearing impairment.

orthopedic: having to do with the bones, muscles, and joints used in movement.

paralysis: loss or impairment of movement, feeling, or function of a part of the body.

paraplegia: paralysis of the lower part of the body, usually caused by damage to the spinal cord. The injury prevents messages going from the brain to the part of the body that is below the point of damage.

physical disability: a physical impairment that limits a person's activity.

prosthesis: an artificial replacement for a missing body part, such as a hand or a leg.

quadriplegia: a condition of paralysis of the body from the neck down; "quadri" means "four" — all four limbs are affected.

therapy: a method of treating a disease, disorder, disability, or injury. Therapy can include exercise, medication, education, or a combination of these. The purpose of therapy is to cure the disease or disorder or to increase the person's skills when the condition is permanent.

INDEX